Grand Canyon National Park

Captions written by Todd R. Berger, Grand Canyon Association

Photographers – Bob and Suzanne Clemenz, Bryce Canyon National Park, Chuck Lawsen, Dai Hirota, David Elms Jr., Dennis Flaherty, Dick Dietrich, © Ed Callaert/Larry Ulrich Stock, Erwin & Peggy Bauer, George H. H. Huey, John P. George, John Wagner, Jonathan L. Mortenson, Josef Muench, © Patty Thomas/Josiah Davidson Scenic Photography, Keuning Photography, Larry Ulrich, Laurence Parent, R. & N. Bowers, Russ Finley, Stewart Aitchison, © StoneNP/leesonphoto, Tom Danielsen, Tom & Pat Leeson, Tom Till, and William Smithey Jr.

ISBN-13: 978-1-60068-087-8

First Printing, December 2008

© Impact, 4961 Windplay Drive, El Dorado Hills, CA 95762
Printed in China

This book has been produced with the assistance of the Grand Canyon Association, a nonprofit partner that aids Grand Canyon National Park in reaching its scientific and educational goals.
For more information, please visit www.grandcanyon.org.

GRAND CANYON
National Park

Over time, the elements have scoured and carved the dramatically splendid
Grand Canyon, known as one of the world's seven natural wonders.
The distance from the South Rim to the North Rim varies from half a mile
(0.8 km) to eighteen miles (29 km), and the canyon has a maximum depth
of 6,000 feet (1,800 m). This great range in elevation allows for a variety of
climate, flora, and fauna; of the seven life zones on the North American
continent, four can be experienced within the Grand Canyon.

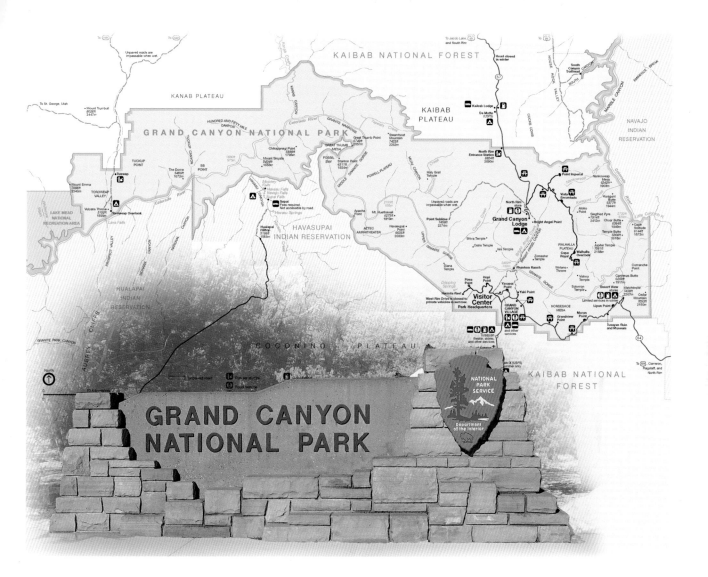

Grand Canyon Lodge on the North Rim is the second lodge to be built near Bright Angel Point. The first, built in 1928, succumbed to fire in 1932. The new lodge, which was completed in 1937 and still stands today, offers dining with a canyon view and the best veranda on either rim for lazy afternoon canyon-watching.

Angels Window is a natural arch in the North Rim's Kaibab Limestone near Cape Royal. Windows tend to be arches that are high on a rock wall. Angels Window sits at an elevation approaching 7,700 feet (2,350 m).

This view from the North Rim near Bright Angel Point shows the three major temples—(left to right) Deva, Brahma, and Zoroaster—which tower over Bright Angel Canyon and the North Kaibab Trail as they descend to the Colorado River. In the Grand Canyon, narrow buttes topped by a caprock of yellow Coconino Sandstone are known as temples.

The view from the North Rim's Cape Royal reveals the South Rim on the horizon and the rock formation known as Wotans Throne (center, top), named after the chief god in German mythology. Cape Royal lies some 25 miles (40 km) from the North Rim developed area at the end of Cape Royal Road.

Cape Royal on the North Rim and the eastern Grand Canyon are visible from Moran Point on the South Rim. The point is named for Thomas Moran, an artist whose early work inspired federal lawmakers to create Yellowstone National Park, the world's first such park. But he also painted the Grand Canyon, including *The Chasm of the Colorado* (1874), which was purchased by Congress for $10,000 and was originally hung in the U.S. Capitol.

Sunrise seen from the North Rim's Point Imperial illuminates Mount Hayden (bottom right), Marble Canyon, and on the horizon, the western reaches of the Navajo Nation. Navajos are one of many tribes with spiritual and cultural ties to the Grand Canyon.

This view from the Transept Trail shows the changing fall colors of a North Rim forest, with ponderosa pine, quaking aspen, and Gambel oak shining ostentatiously in the late afternoon sun. In comparison to the South Rim, the North Rim has cooler temperatures and greater precipitation, allowing many types of deciduous trees to thrive. The San Francisco Peaks near Flagstaff are visible on the horizon.

Grand Canyon National Park has large forests containing several different tree species. Among the most common (clockwise from top left) are ponderosa pine, found on both rims; Utah juniper, which can be seen primarily on the South Rim and in the canyon; pinyon pine, also occurring primarily on the South Rim and in the canyon; and quaking aspen, which grows almost exclusively on the North Rim.

The park is home to dozens of mammal species. (Clockwise from top left) Commonly out and about only at night, ringtails will take a keen interest in food packs left on the ground. Within the park, the Kaibab squirrel, with its distinctive tasseled ears and snow-white tail, lives only on the North Rim. Smaller than mountain lions, bobcats are also more abundant within the park—although they tend to hunt at night and avoid people, so it is rare to encounter one. Agile desert bighorns prefer the safety of the rocky cliffs of the inner canyon and only rarely venture onto the rims.

(Clockwise from top left) Coyotes can be seen on both rims and in the canyon in search of jackrabbits and rodents for dinner. Mule deer, with their oversize ears and black-tipped tails, are common on both rims and can even be found deep within the canyon. The exact number of mountain lions in the national park is unknown, although they are extremely rare and are almost never seen by humans. The silver on top and rust-colored on the bottom gray fox is a citizen of both rims.

Trains first reached the South Rim of the Grand Canyon in September 1901. The arrival of the train shortened the time needed to reach the South Rim from a matter of days to a matter of hours, and visitation increased considerably after 1901. But as with most of America, people slowly gravitated toward automobiles to reach the park, and by 1969, the passenger train line from Williams to the park had shut down. New investors rebuilt the tracks and restored vintage steam engines, diesel locomotives, and historic passenger cars, and by September 1989, the Grand Canyon Railway began carrying a new generation of passengers to the park. Today, hundreds of thousands of tourists visit the park by train.

The Desert View Watchtower stands near the eastern edge of Grand Canyon National Park. Mary Colter, who designed many of the buildings in Grand Canyon Village and at Phantom Ranch, designed the Watchtower to resemble towers built by prehistoric peoples in the Southwest. The tower was completed in 1932.

Vaseys Paradise along the Colorado River in eastern Grand Canyon is a verdant spring in an otherwise stark desert landscape. The waterfall pours from the Redwall Limestone walls of Marble Canyon, and the water sustains a lush variety of plants, including redbud trees, cardinal monkeyflowers, and maidenhair ferns.

(Left to right) Poisonous-yet-pretty sacred datura blooms in the inner canyon from May to October. Desert globe mallow thrives in arid, sun-baked conditions in the canyon and occasionally on the rims. Scarlet monkeyflower needs plenty of water to thrive, but it can be found around seeps, near springs and along creeks in the canyon.

The Palisades of the Desert (seen here from Desert View) are a towering wall of cliffs that were said to resemble a "palisade," a fence with closely spaced, pointed stakes.

The Palisades of the Desert (seen here from Desert View are a towering wall of cliffs that were said to resemble a "palisade," a fence with closely spaced, pointed stakes.

Lightning strikes are common at the Grand Canyon during the monsoon season from early July to mid-September. Runoff from drenching thundershowers over millions of years has helped carve the canyon.

Rainbows make occasional appearances over the Grand Canyon, particularly during monsoon season between early July and mid-September. Those lucky enough to see one are often treated to an almost gaudy display of color from the bottom of the canyon high into the sky.

Looking west from a spot near the South Rim's Yaki Point, one can see O'Neill Butte (the red formation in the right, bottom corner) traversed by the South Kaibab Trail, Plateau Point and the Plateau Point Trail just above O'Neill Butte, and Havasupai Point (on the horizon just left of center), home of the South Bass trailhead.

The Grand Canyon is one of the seven natural wonders of the world. It extends 277 river miles (446 km) through northern Arizona, a distance 50 miles (80 km) longer than the drive from Grand Canyon Village to Phoenix.

One of the most amazing things visitors to the Grand Canyon notice is that the canyon changes color, sometimes before your eyes. The colors you see depend on the time of day, time of year, cloud cover, atmospheric conditions, and haze.

Looking northwest from Lipan Point on the South Rim, a grand expanse of the canyon is visible on the horizon. Named after the Lipan Tribe of Texas by cartographer Francois Matthes in 1902, the point is a particularly good spot for sunset viewing.

John Wesley Powell led the first formal expedition to explore the Grand Canyon of the Colorado River. Powell's expedition pushed off on May 24, 1869 at Green River, Wyoming. They reached the mouth of the Virgin River (today beneath Lake Mead) on August 30, 1869, marking the first successful voyage through "the Great Unknown."

Pinnacles, buttes, temples, and mesas create the undulating topography of the Grand Canyon. Most of the formations, including this pinnacle of Kaibab Limestone near the South Rim, result from differing rates of erosion: as erosion carries away the surrounding rock, the more-resistant rock formation is left behind.

Hopi House, completed in 1905, is modeled after the ancient structures in the village of Oraibi on the Hopi Mesas to the east of the national park. Native stone and wood provided the building materials, and Hopi builders worked on most of the construction. Designed by architect Mary Colter, the building still serves its original purpose as a sales outlet for American Indian crafts and artwork.

The Santa Fe Railway opened El Tovar Hotel in 1905 with a desire to bring a high level of luxury to then-rustic Grand Canyon Village. The hotel is named after Pedro de Tovar, one of the explorers on Francisco Vásquez de Coronado's 1540 expedition to the Southwest.

The South Rim's Lookout Studio (upper left) has an enviable perch overlooking the canyon. Built in 1914, the curio and gift shop was meant to compete with Kolb Studio just to the west. Still selling gifts, the Kaibab Limestone structure blends into its surroundings and offers some of the best California condor viewing from its outdoor patios on the canyon side of the building.

The fireplace under the vaulted ceiling of Hermits Rest warms many a chilly traveler. The building, erected in 1914, was designed to look as if built by an unskilled "hermit," and it blends in perfectly with its rocky, forested surroundings. The rustic building is one of eight historic buildings still standing in Grand Canyon National Park designed by architect Mary Colter.

(Clockwise from top left) Steller's jays, common to both rims, are unmistakable with their black-crowned heads and radiant blue plumage. Great horned owls live throughout the park and can occasionally be heard—though rarely seen. California condors were once nearly extinct, but captive-breeding programs are helping these giant birds recover, including the more than 60 condors in the Grand Canyon region. Common ravens can be seen just about everywhere in the park; these highly intelligent, opportunistic birds will easily find their way into food packs.

A mule train descends the Bright Angel Trail. Mule wranglers have been taking paying tourists into the Grand Canyon on muleback since at least 1887, when "Captain" John Hance first advertised this service in a Flagstaff newspaper. Mules have also been used for mining and packing all kinds of things in and out of the canyon, including ore from once-thriving inner-canyon mines, the mail to and from Supai, and all the supplies—from bed linens to steaks—needed by Phantom Ranch at the bottom of the canyon.

The Silver Bridge over the Colorado River connects the North Kaibab Trail to the River Trail, as well as supports the transcanyon pipeline that supplies water to the South Rim. The bridge is a familiar site for hikers headed to Phantom Ranch via the Bright Angel Trail, but mule riders cross a little farther upriver on the Kaibab Suspension Bridge.

Havasu Falls is in the Grand Canyon, but not in the national park. The famous blue-green waters of Havasu Creek and its namesake waterfall run through the Havasupai Indian Reservation, which abuts the borders of Grand Canyon National Park to the southwest. The reservation has a beautiful campground below the falls along the creek, and the nearby Havasupai village of Supai features the last post office in the United States to receive and send all of its mail by horse or mule.

When looking at the Grand Canyon from the bottom along the banks of the Colorado River, it hardly seems like the same place seen from the rims. The igneous rock, morphed by long-ago, deep-under-the-earth heat and pressure, is black with curvy striations of beige and pink. The view is narrower in most places, with only the walls of the Inner Gorge and the sky visible when you look up.

The ancestral Puebloan people used granaries hundreds of feet above the Colorado River to store food out of reach from rodents and sheltered from the elements. These granaries along the river near Nankoweap Canyon were used between AD 1050 and AD 1150.

From Toroweap Point, the volcanic cinder cone known as Vulcans Throne is just visible in the upper left of this photograph. The western Grand Canyon includes many cinder cones, lava flows, and remnants of lava dams. Lava dams have blocked the Colorado River at several times in the distant past, contributing to the formation of the Grand Canyon.